D1237584

Dream BIG

American Idol SUPERSTARS

Kellie Pickler

Hal Marcovitz

Mason Crest Publishers

Produced by 21st Century Publishing and Communications, Inc.

MASON CREST PUBLISHERS INC.
370 Reed Road
Broomall, Pennsylvania 19008
(866) MCP-BOOK (toll free)
www.masoncrest.com

Printed in the United States of America.

First Printing

9 8 7 6 5 4 3 2 1

Library of Congress Cataloging-in-Publication Data

Marcovitz, Hal.
Kellie Pickler / Hal Marcovitz.
p. cm. — (Dream big: American idol superstars)
Includes bibliographical references and index.
ISBN 978-1-4222-1510-4 (hardback : alk. paper)
ISBN 978-1-4222-1603-3 (pbk. : alk. paper)
1. Pickler, Kellie, 1986– —Juvenile literature. 2. Singers—United States—Biography—Juvenile literature. I. Title.
ML3930.P465M37 2010
782.42164092—dc22
[B] 2009022764

Publisher's notes:
All quotations in this book come from original sources, and contain the spelling and grammatical inconsistencies of the original text.

The Web sites mentioned in this book were active at the time of publication. The publisher is not responsible for Web sites that have changed their addresses or discontinued operation since the date of publication. The publisher will review and update the Web site addresses each time the book is reprinted.

Contents

American Idol TIMELINE

October 5, 2001
Pop Idol, a TV reality show created by Simon Fuller, debuts in the United Kingdom and becomes a smash hit.

Fall 2001
Based on the success of *Pop Idol*, and after initially rejecting the concept, FOX Network agrees to buy *American Idol*, a national talent competition and TV reality show.

Spring 2002
Auditions for *American Idol* Season 1 are held in New York City, Los Angeles, Chicago, Dallas, Miami, Atlanta, and Seattle.

January 21, 2003
American Idol Season 2 premieres without Brian Dunkleman, leaving Ryan Seacrest as the sole host.

May 21, 2003
- *American Idol* Season 2 finale airs.
- Ruben Studdard narrowly wins and Clay Aiken is the runner-up.
- Runner-up Clay Aiken goes on to become extremely successful both critically and commercially.

January 19, 2004
American Idol Season 3 premieres.

2001 2002 2003 2004

June 11, 2002
American Idol Season 1 premieres on FOX Network, with Simon Cowell, Paula Abdul, and Randy Jackson as the judges, and Ryan Seacrest and Brian Dunkleman as the co-hosts.

September 4, 2002
- *American Idol* Season 1 finale airs.
- Kelly Clarkson wins and Justin Guarini is the runner-up.
- Kelly Clarkson goes on to become the most successful Idol winner and a superstar in the music industry.

Fall 2002
Auditions for *American Idol* Season 2 are held in New York City, Los Angeles, Miami, Detroit, Nashville, and Austin.

January 27, 2004
William Hung's audition is aired and his humble response to Simon Cowell's scathing criticism make William the most famous American Idol non-qualifier and earn him record deals and a cult-like following.

April 21, 2004
Jennifer Hudson is voted off the show in 7th place, and goes on to win the role of Effie in *Dreamgirls*, for which she wins an Academy Award, a Golden Globe Award, and a Grammy Award.

May 26, 2004
- *American Idol* Season 3 finale airs with 65 million viewers casting their votes.
- Fantasia Barrino is crowned the winner and Diana DeGarmo is the runner-up.
- Fantasia soon becomes the first artist in the history of Billboard to debut at number one with her first single.

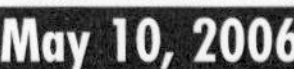

May 10, 2006
Chris Daughtry is voted off the show in 4th place, and soon after forms the band, Daughtry, and releases its debut album, which becomes number one on the charts, wins many awards, and finds huge commercial success.

April 26, 2006
Kellie Pickler is voted off the show in 6th place, and soon releases her debut album, which rockets to number one on the Billboard Top Country Album chart.

January 17, 2006
American Idol Season 5 premieres and for the first time airs in high definition.

May 24, 2006
- *American Idol* Season 5 finale airs.
- Taylor Hicks is the winner and Katharine McPhee the runner-up.
- Elliot Yamin, the second runner-up, goes on to release his debut album, which goes gold.

January 16, 2007
American Idol Season 6 premieres.

April 2007
The *American Idol* Songwriting Contest is announced.

January 15, 2008
American Idol Season 7 airs with a four-hour two-day premiere.

April 9, 2008
Idol Gives Back returns for its second year.

May 21, 2008
- *American Idol* Season 7 finale airs.
- David Cook wins with 54.6 million votes and David Archuleta is the runner-up with 42.9 million votes.
- Both Davids go on to tremendous post-Idol success with successful albums and singles.

2005 2006 2007 2008 2009

May 25, 2005
- *American Idol* Season 4 finale airs.
- Carrie Underwood wins and Bo Bice is the runner-up.
- Carrie goes on to become one of the most successful Idol winners, selling millions of albums and winning scores of major awards.

January 18, 2005
- *American Idol* Season 4 premieres.
- Some rules change:
  - The age limit is raised from 24 to 28.
  - The semi-final competition is separated by gender up until the 12 finalists.

April 24–25, 2007
American Idol Gives Back, a charitable campaign to raise money for underprivileged children worldwide, airs, and raises more than $70 million.

May 23, 2007
- *American Idol* Season 6 finale airs.
- Jordin Sparks wins with 74 million votes and Blake Lewis is the runner-up.
- Jordin goes on to join Kelly Clarkson and Carrie Underwood in the ranks of highly successful post-Idol recording artists.

January 13, 2009
American Idol Season 8 premieres adding Kara DioGuardi as a fourth judge.

February 14, 2009
The American Idol Experience, a theme park attraction, officially opens at Disney's Hollywood Studio in Florida.

May 20, 2009
- *American Idol* Season 8 finale airs.
- Kris Allen unexpectedly wins and Adam Lambert is the runner-up.
- Almost 100 million people voted in the season 8 finale.

Kellie Pickler gets emotional as she sings her hit song "I Wonder" at the 2007 CMA Music Festival. A few months later at the Country Music Awards ceremony, Kellie broke down crying while performing the song, which won her Performance of the Year from Country Music Television Awards.

Performance of the Year

As Kellie Pickler took the stage at the 2007 Country Music Awards, she planned to belt out a vibrant performance of "I Wonder," the hit song from her debut album that established her as a top country music star. But as she made her way through the song, audience members were stunned to see her eyes welling up in tears.

Kellie wrote the song as a tribute to her mother, Cynthia, who lived in an abusive relationship with Kellie's father, Bo. The situation at the Pickler home was so bad that when Kellie was very young her mother had to leave her in the care of Kellie's grandparents. That is the story Kellie chose to tell when she wrote "I Wonder."

All those emotions and memories found their way back to Kellie's mind as she performed "I Wonder" during the nationally televised awards show. In fact, she was barely able to end the song, choking on the final few **lyrics**. Later, she said,

> **"That should have been one of the most magical nights of my life, career-wise. But in my personal life, I was so depressed. I was going through a breakup, which was bad enough. Then, right before I was to go on stage I got a call from someone back home telling me that my mother had shown up. . . . It was all too much, and I just broke down on stage."**

Topping the Charts

About a year before Kellie performed at the Country Music Awards, she had been a contestant on *American Idol*, the enormously popular TV series in which unknown performers vie for a recording contract. For the winner, stardom is virtually guaranteed. Kellie did not win—in fact, in the 2006 competition she did no better than sixth place.

Still, there was no denying her talent and appeal to members of the audience. Soon after she was voted off *Idol*, Kellie signed a recording contract and got down to work on her debut album, which was titled *Small Town Girl*.

As the name of the album suggests, its songs describe what life was like for Kellie growing up in a small town in North Carolina in a family broken up by abuse and turmoil. Another song on the album, "My Angel," was dedicated to her grandmother, who helped raise her. "I dedicated the album to my grandmother, and wanted that song to close the album," Kellie said.

No Dream Too Big

When the album was released in late 2006, it shot to the top of the country charts. *Small Town Girl* was certified gold in early

Kellie celebrates her two ASCAP awards for Most Performed Songs. In her acceptance speech in Nashville in 2008, she encouraged hopeful performers to use their life experiences to become stronger. Kellie reminded them to follow their dreams, no matter how big, just as she had.

2007, and some of the singles from the album garnered important music industry awards. For example, in 2008 "I Wonder" and another single from the album, "Red High Heels," won recognition as Most Performed Songs by ASCAP, the professional association that represents songwriters and composers. Kellie accepted the ASCAP awards at a gala ceremony in Nashville, Tennessee, the capital of country music. Said Kellie,

> **"What I've learned the last year is that no dream is too big. You can let things bring you down or you can use them to make you stronger. I used everything that has happened to me as fuel to get me where I am today. You can't give up on your dreams 'cause sometimes, that's all you have."**

WHAT IS ASCAP?

ASCAP stands for the American Society of Composers, Authors, and Publishers. Each year, ASCAP confers awards to songwriters in a number of musical categories, including pop, soul, film and TV scores, Latin, country, hip-hop, and rock.

ASCAP was founded in 1914 by some of America's top songwriters and composers of the era, including Irving Berlin, Jerome Kern, Victor Herbert, and John Philip Sousa. Today, there are more than 350,000 members of ASCAP.

Emotional Performance

"I Wonder" also garnered awards from Country Music Television, the TV network devoted to country and western music. The video Kellie made for the song won awards as Breakthrough Video of the Year as well as Tearjerker Video of the Year. Also, Country Music Television honored Kellie for the emotional performance of the song she gave at the Country Music Awards show, voting it Performance of the Year.

Kellie was unable to attend the Country Music Television awards show in Nashville because she was on tour at the time, performing in Scottsdale, Arizona. Still, the producers of the show arranged for a **satellite hookup** between Nashville and

Kellie always puts her emotions into every performance. The video Kellie made of "I Wonder" won Country Music Television awards as Tearjerker Video of the Year and Breakthrough Video of the Year. When she accepted the Breakthrough Video award, Kellie thanked *American Idol* for helping launch her musical career.

Scottsdale so that Kellie could still accept her awards and make a short speech. In accepting the award for Breakthrough Video, Kellie said,

> **"Oh my gosh! This is the first time I've ever won anything in my life. I'm so excited I don't know what to say. Thank you, *American Idol*. You are the rocket that launched my career."**

Kellie grew up in North Carolina and considers herself a small-town girl. She credits her grandmother for introducing her to music by singing church hymns with her in the evenings on the porch swing. Later Kellie sang along with records by country stars like LeAnn Rimes and Faith Hill.

2

A Real Small Town Girl

As a young girl, Kellie often sat on the front porch swing with her grandmother Faye Pickler, who loved to sing old church hymns—"Amazing Grace" and "Jesus Loves Me." Kellie listened closely, soon learning the words and then singing along. For Kellie, those early evenings on the porch swing were special times.

There wasn't much money in the Pickler home, certainly not enough to afford expensive music and singing lessons for Kellie. The future star of *American Idol* and the country music charts learned all she would need to know about singing on the front porch of her grandparents' home in rural North Carolina. Recalls Kellie,

"My grandmother . . . had a collection of children's books, and one of those was a songbook. We would sit on the swing on the front porch, and I would just sing my heart out. . . . When I was a little older, my grand-parents bought me a little boom box, and I sang along with LeAnn Rimes, Shania [Twain], Faith [Hill], Tammy Wynette, and especially Dolly Parton. I have always loved Dolly Parton, I felt like we had something in common. We both came from nothing, and had big, big dreams."

INSPIRED BY DOLLY PARTON

Kellie's main inspiration is Dolly Parton, the veteran country singer who has also made her mark as a film actress and song-writer. Dolly started singing as a young girl and has gone on to become the most successful female artist in country music history, releasing more than 60 albums in a recording career that began in 1967. She is also a gifted musician who has mastered the guitar, banjo, piano, harmonica, drums, and fiddle.

Kellie says she admires Dolly for her versatility. "I am the biggest Dolly Parton fan," says Kellie. "I love her songwriting. She's a great singer, a great performer. She can act. She's the whole package, and the personality is the icing on the cake. I think she's great, and I can only hope to follow in her footsteps."

She also admires Dolly for overcoming adversity as a young girl—much the same way Kellie has had to overcome an unhappy childhood. Dolly was born into severe poverty in rural Tennessee, one of 12 children. Says Kellie, "I think it's great that someone like her who has had to over-come family obstacles like she has . . . can still walk around with a smile on her face."

Class Clown

Kellie was born in Albemarle, North Carolina, on June 28, 1986. Her earliest years were marked by turmoil because her mother,

Kellie was especially inspired by Dolly Parton, a gifted musician and songwriter who has released more than 60 albums over a long, successful career. Kellie has always felt a connection with Dolly because both women grew up poor and overcame difficult childhoods.

Cynthia, and father, Bo, were constantly fighting. Bo Pickler struggled with alcohol and drug abuse. Soon, her mother, who was abused by Bo, had to abandon Kellie, leaving her in the care of Kellie's grandparents. Clyde and Fay Pickler loved Kellie deeply, raising her in the small town of Palestine. Bo was eventually sent to prison, while Cynthia had little to do with her daughter.

Kellie's talent emerged in her high school years. She enjoyed performing in front of people and would dive into whatever high school activity that would give her the chance to appear in front

Kellie was always outgoing as a teen and loved to perform in front of a crowd. But she couldn't decide on a career path after high school and later became a roller-skating waitress. Luckily she found a way out of her boring jobs when she auditioned for *American Idol.*

of an audience. She particularly enjoyed drama club, cheerleading, and gymnastics. She says,

> **"I've always been comfortable in front of people. I've always been the joker, the class clown. Music and laughter is how I dealt with everything. I'd rather laugh about it than cry about it."**

Uncertain Future

In 2002, when Kellie was a sophomore at North Stanly High School, she was devastated by the death of her grandmother Faye. "She was always there for me, and then she was gone," Kellie says.

Two years later, as Kellie prepared to graduate from high school, she was unsure of what to do with the rest of her life. Her grandfather was a hard-working electrician, but he could not afford to send her to college.

At the age of 17 Kellie entered the Miss Stanly County beauty pageant and won—her talent was singing. Winning the local pageant gave her a chance to move on to the Miss North Carolina competition, but she fell short of taking that crown. Still, first prize in the Miss Stanly County pageant was full **tuition** at the local community college.

Kellie enrolled with the goal of becoming a **cosmetologist**, but dropped out just before graduation after realizing that she found hairstyling boring. Besides, she didn't want to work in a job that would force her to be cooped up inside four walls. She says, "I hated it. I was miserable, being in the classroom everyday, four walls could not hold me in. I was only lacking a few [courses] when I quit."

After dropping out of community college, she briefly took classes in nursing and **paralegal** studies and also found a job as a roller-skating waitress at a Sonic Drive-In while deciding which path to take with her life. She says,

> **"I've seen my whole family struggle—with money, with relationships, with alcohol, and I thought there must be a better way. I wasn't sure how I would get out, but I knew I would."**

During her *Idol* audition, Kellie impressed Simon, Randy, and Paula with her rendition of Kelly Clarkson's "Since U Been Gone." But equally important was her adorable personality and Southern charm. Soon she was a favorite of the three judges, audiences, and music critics across the country.

3

Full of Southern Charm

A friend had told Kellie that *American Idol* planned to hold auditions in nearby Greensboro, North Carolina. Kellie soon decided to audition, and found herself waiting in line with thousands of other singers who hoped to impress judges Simon Cowell, Paula Abdul, and Randy Jackson. Kellie made it through the preliminary auditions before the show's producers, and was then invited in to perform before Simon, Paula, and Randy.

When Kellie tried out for *American Idol*, she set the bar high for herself—choosing Kelly Clarkson's hit "Since U Been Gone" for her audition song. Kelly had been the winner of *Idol*'s first season. "I know I've got big shoes to fill, that's for sure," Kellie told the judges.

After singing just a few bars of "Since U Been Gone," Kellie was pleased that the judges were impressed. Paula said, "You're adorable. I like the conviction in your voice. I like you."

Paula and the other judges voted unanimously to send Kellie to Hollywood. In addition to being impressed by Kellie's stunning performance, the judges also admitted to being smitten by her bubbly personality. As they were trying to give her constructive criticism, Kellie insisted on interrupting them, telling the judges how excited she was and how she couldn't wait to tell her grandfather about the audition. Instead of being annoyed, Simon, Paula, and Randy found Kellie's girlishness charming. As Kellie dashed out of the audition room, Simon said,

> **"That's a nice girl. That's the one I'd like to see do well."**

SIMON COWELL, NICE GUY

Kellie's on-air exchanges with Simon resulted in a lot of laughs, making her one of the few *American Idol* competitors to get Simon to show his lighter side. Otherwise, Simon has developed a reputation as a tough judge whose sarcastic remarks often leave *Idol* competitors trembling in fear.

But Simon says he is really just a victim of his own reputation and that off camera, he's really quite a nice guy. In fact, he says, many *Idol* contestants are actually disappointed when he *doesn't* insult them. He says,

> **"People come up to me and sing, and I say, 'That was great. Thank you.' And they're like, 'Well, aren't you going to be rude to me?' No. 'Well, can you be rude to me?' No! When I miss auditions, contestants get upset that I'm not there, because they expect me to be cruel to them—it's some sort of badge of honor. That's how crazy everything is."**

Not Just Singing

Once the competition got underway in Hollywood, the fifth season of *Idol* soon shaped up as the most competitive ever. In addition to Kellie, that year's performers included Elliott Yamin, Ace Young, Katharine McPhee, Mandisa, Chris Daughtry, Bucky Covington, and Taylor Hicks. Kellie became an audience favorite, not only because of her singing talent but also because of her on-air flubs and humorous exchanges with the judges, particularly Simon. She regularly mispronounced words and misunderstood what the judges were trying to tell her.

Kellie (in yellow) appears with the other top 12 contestants of *American Idol* season five. The group was unusually talented, and the contest became the fiercest to date. In addition to Kellie, several competitors later went on to successful music careers.

Simon wasn't the only one who found Kellie's personality engaging. Wrote *Rolling Stone* music critic Jenny Eliscu,

> **"Kellie Pickler [is] proof that *Idol* isn't just about singing. . . . North Carolina gal Pickler, 19, stands a shot at winning largely on the basis of her wide-eyed-Southern-chick-takes-Hollywood charm. . . . If she picks tough songs and nails a couple of them, she'll be a contender."**

American Idol judges Randy Jackson, Simon Cowell, and Paula Abdul all have distinctive personalities on the show. Although Simon has a reputation for being a harsh critic, Kellie was one of the few contestants who got him to show his sense of humor.

Not Another TV Talent Show

American Idol was not the first talent show to air on American TV. The *Major Bowes Amateur Hour* premiered on radio back in the 1930s; in 1948, the show transitioned to TV as the *Original Amateur Hour* with talent scout Ted Mack as host. *Amateur Hour* managed to remain on the air into the 1970s and was even revived in the 1990s as the *New Original Amateur Hour.* A similar program, which aired in the 1980s and 1990s, was titled *Star Search.*

What set *American Idol* apart from these prior TV talent shows was its audience participation. For the *Amateur Hour* and *Star Search* programs, winners were picked by panels of judges, although in *Star Search* the **studio audience** also had a vote in the finals. In *American Idol*, the judges certainly have a strong influence on the outcome, but the ultimate decisions are made by the viewers at home, who can call in their votes. In the year in which Kellie competed, more than 63 million votes were cast in the final round.

American Idol is based on its British version, *Pop Idol*, which premiered in 2000. The concept is simple: unknown singers compete in elimination rounds week after week until a winner emerges. Wrote *Newsweek* magazine,

> **"You thought this was just another TV talent show. Well, it is—except that *American Idol* is also one of those addictive, unpredictable, heartbreaking programs that come around about as often as a leap year. The secrets to its success are wonderfully simple. First, there's the fact that the viewers vote for the winner. It's an ingenious way to get us empathizing—make that obsessing—with these contestants to the point where we fall in love with them, spending hours phoning in or text-messaging our all-important votes."**

Rocky Beginning

Actually, the show had a rather rocky beginning. After its debut on British TV, the show's creators, Simon Cowell and English music producer Simon Fuller (he discovered the Spice Girls) offered the show to a number of American TV networks but were repeatedly turned down. Simon Cowell recalls sitting in meeting after meeting with American TV executives, who were unimpressed with the idea for the show. Says Simon,

> **"I was thrown out in one pitch meeting. After 30 seconds, the guy told me to get out. The main thing we were being told was music doesn't work on TV in prime time. We tried to explain that there's a lot more than music on the show."**

Eventually, the hunt for an American TV network came to an end when one of *Pop Idol*'s biggest fans, Elisabeth Murdoch, convinced her father to buy the rights to air the show on

LOST IN TRANSLATION?

Versions of *Idol* can be seen in some 35 countries in North America, South America, Europe, and Asia. In Bulgaria, the show is called *Music Idol*. That's also the show's name in Rumania. In Turkey, the show is named *Turkstar*. In France, viewers tune in to *Nouvelle Star*. In Greece, the show is called *Super Idol*. In Poland, it's simply called *Idol*. All the versions have their own judges, performers, and, of course, dramatic conclusions.

They also have their own humorous moments. One of the most infamous occurred on the Rumanian version when a contestant auditioned by singing the Mariah Carey hit "Without You." The song includes several repetitions of the lyrics "I can't live . . . " which the English-challenged contestant misinterpreted as the name "Ken Lee." As she continued to sing "Ken Lee . . . Ken Lee . . . " the Rumanian judges found it hard to contain their laughter.

Simon Fuller, the founder of 19 Entertainment, teamed with Simon Cowell to bring Britain's *Pop Idol* to America. TV executives were not impressed with the idea of a musical competition in prime time. Finally the Fox Network bought the rights to the show, and the rest is ratings history.

American TV. Elisabeth's father, Rupert Murdoch, is the head of the company that owns the Fox TV network.

Idol Catches Fire

After that somewhat bumpy start, the show caught fire, with some 50 million viewers a week tuning in. The first season was highlighted by a spirited competition between Kelly Clarkson and Justin Guarini. In the second year, another dramatic competition was staged with rhythm and blues singer Ruben Studdard emerging as the winner, but the runner-up, Clay Aiken, has gone on to enjoy a career as a recording artist and stage actor. He began a trend that would be followed by other *Idol* competitors: finishing strongly in the competition and establishing a fan base could also lead to a big-time career in entertainment.

Other top talents discovered by the show include the season four winner, country star Carrie Underwood, and season three competitor Jennifer Hudson, who fell short of winning but, nevertheless, has won an Academy Award and released a top-selling album.

***Idol*'s second season runner-up Clay Aiken has released four albums, including *On My Way Here* in 2008. Clay started a trend among *Idol* competitors: making the finals, but not winning, and going on to an acclaimed career in music and acting.**

Top-Rated Show

Other competitors have fallen short of achieving stardom, but *American Idol* has opened many doors for them. They have become busy entertainers, recording albums and giving their fans opportunities to see them on stage and screen.

Rocker Bo Bice, who finished in second place behind Carrie in season 4, tours with his band, has written music for movies, and has recorded a gold-certified album, *The Real Thing*. Constantine Maroulis, who competed against Carrie and Bo, has appeared on **Broadway**. Diana DeGarmo, who finished second to Fantasia Barrino in season three, has also appeared on Broadway. LaToya London, who competed against Fantasia and Diana, has toured in stage productions. Commenting on the enormous popularity of the *Idol* contestants—whether they win or lose—*Time* magazine said,

> **"The show draws viewers from grade school through retirement, which is unusual for TV today. For the kids, it serves up a steady stream of fresh pop faces. For their parents and grandparents, the oldies playlist offers an idealized past. . . . What draws us through *Idol's* corniness—the embarrassing musical commercials, the results shows that cram 30 seconds of suspense into an hour—is the singers. Over a season, we learn their quirks, struggles, weaknesses and family stories."**

With so many *Idol* performers going on to successful careers in the arts, the show has definitely found a place in American popular culture. Each year in which it has aired, *Idol* has remained Fox's top-rated show.

Image Change

Flubs and misunderstandings aside, Kellie was clearly emerging as one of the favorites to win the competition. Said *USA Today*, "She's so full of Southern charm that she's practically batter-dipped and honey-glazed." Even Simon predicted that Kellie had the potential to win, suggesting that he liked her better than Carrie, who had won the year before. Meanwhile, the competition was fierce as Taylor, Katharine, Chris, and Elliott were each scoring highly among the judges while earning big votes from audience members.

Kellie entered the competition as a country singer, and she relied on that **genre** for several weeks of the contest, turning in strong performances of Martina McBride's "How Far," Patsy Cline's "Walkin' After Midnight," and Reba McEntire's "Fancy." In *American Idol*, though, the competitors must also be able to sing outside their strongest genres. Each week, the producers select a theme.

On April 11, the producers selected songs from the 1970s rock band Queen as the genre of the week. Kellie decided to perform "Bohemian Rhapsody," an edgy song in which the singer relives a nightmare. To perform the song, Kellie broke out of her innocent country girl character. She wore a black leather jacket, tight black slacks, and black high heels. *USA Today* called Kellie's performance "fierce . . . pulling off a radical image change."

CHRIS DAUGHTRY

With just a few weeks left in the season five competition, *Entertainment Weekly* picked Chris Daughtry as the favorite to win *American Idol*. Chris, a hard-rocking singer who also grew up in North Carolina, had amassed a large devoted fan base since the competition started months before. But Chris's successful run on *American Idol* came to a shocking conclusion in early May. After Chris performed stirring covers of two Elvis Presley hits, he was unexpectadly voted off the show.

Following his departure from *Idol*, Chris has gone on to a very successful career as a recording artist. His album, *Daughtry*, sold more than 4 million copes and was certified by *Billboard* magazine as the top selling album of 2007. He has also toured and made many appearances on TV, including a non-singing role in the crime drama *CSI: NY*.

Kellie offers a different style and sound during one of her later *Idol* performances. After relying on her strength as an innocent-looking country singer, she changed her image and wowed the audience with her rendition of the edgy rock ballad "Bohemian Rhapsody."

Kellie gives her last performance before being voted off *American Idol.* After two uninspired numbers, both the judges and audience decided it was time for her to go. But even though Kellie didn't win the contest, her taste of success inspired her to keep working toward a career in music.

Bland Performance

That type of enthusiasm for Kellie's performances would soon die down. A week after her knockout performance of "Bohemian Rhapsody," Kellie gave a half-hearted performance of the Frank Sinatra love song "Bewitched, Bothered, and Bewildered." Kellie was saved from elimination, probably because Ace had an even worse week, flubbing a performance of Rod Stewart's "That's All."

For Kellie, the end finally came on April 26 after she turned in a bland performance of "Unchained Melody" by the Righteous Brothers, and the audience responded by voting her out of the competition. "You were like a robot," Simon huffed. Kellie freely admitted,

> **"I deserved to get the boot this week. I probably should have gotten it last week, but I'm grateful that the fans let me have another week. I had bad performances back to back. There's no excuse."**

Following Kellie's departure, the competition continued for another four weeks. Chris seemed to have the edge but was shocked to be voted out of the competition two weeks after Kellie. On May 24, the competition came down to the final two contestants, with Taylor edging Katharine to win the title. By then, Kellie had already returned to North Carolina, but she didn't intend to stay home long. She had big plans for the future.

After *Idol,* Kellie went back to her small town, but she had lots of plans for her future. She soon signed a record contract and moved to Nashville. She also made TV appearances and went on a hectic *post*-Idol tour with fellow competitors—now friends—from season five.

4

Small Town Girl, Big Plans

Kellie may have been voted out of the *American Idol* competition but she had no intention of returning to her former job as a roller-skating waitress. *American Idol's* producer, 19 Entertainment, moved quickly to sign Kellie to a recording contract. She soon packed up and headed for Nashville—even driving the rented U-Haul truck herself.

She picked Nashville as her new home because the city is the center of the country music industry—all the major country **labels** are located there. Moving to Nashville would mean moving away from her grandfather and childhood friends, but

Kellie was anxious to turn the next page in her life. While packing up her belongings, Kellie said,

> **"I came across photos from when I went to audition for *American Idol,* when I was standing in line with all those thousands of people in Greensboro. I just started crying. I couldn't believe how things had changed in a year, and how unreal it seemed to be where I am."**

Touring With Friends

In the days following her exit from *American Idol*, Kellie appeared on several TV shows, including *Total Request Live* and *Live With Regis & Kelly*. After Taylor won the competition, Kellie and other stars from the fifth season performed on the post-*American Idol* tour that visits several cities over the course of the summer.

For three months, Kellie and the other *Idol* contestants performed in some 60 shows. "I'm running on adrenaline and Red Bull," Kellie said during the hectic tour, "but it's a lot of fun. We've all become real close." In fact, during the tour, Kellie became close friends with Mandisa. "Mandisa is like the big sister I never had," she said. "We are always in touch."

Kellie worked too hard during the post-*Idol* tour. She strained her voice and was told by a doctor to take a few days off. She said,

> **"Even though I was on vocal rest for shows in Georgia and Florida, I still wanted to say hello to all the fans, so after Bucky performed I would go out and wave to the crowd so everyone knew that I was there and appreciated their support. After that, I would change into all black and a hoodie and I'd sit right in front of the stage and enjoy watching the others perform. And I have to say that they put on a great show!"**

High Marks for Her Album

Finally, the post-*Idol* tour ended and Kellie settled into her new home in Nashville. She also got down to work with some of the best country songwriters in the business to produce the album *Small Town Girl.* In addition to the single "I Wonder," the album also includes other songs that tell of Kellie's experiences growing up without parents.

Critics gave the album high marks. *Billboard* wrote, "This CD is a moving portrait of a small-town girl coming to terms with

Kellie received high praise for her album *Small Town Girl.* Many of the songs rang true with fans because they reflected events in Kellie's life. Three singles, "I Wonder," "Red High Heels," and "Things That Never Cross a Man's Mind," zoomed to the top 20 on the *Billboard* Country Songs chart.

her past and celebrating the promise of her future." And *People* magazine music critic Ericka Souter wrote,

> **"An endearing naïveté helped Kellie Pickler come in sixth on last season's *American Idol*, and the Albemarle, North Carolina, native still works her wide-eyed innocence on her debut album, *Small Town Girl*. . . . She certainly doesn't have the bluesy vocal strength of *Idol*'s other country girl, Carrie Underwood, but**

Kellie sings the national anthem at the 2007 NASCAR Busch Series Orbitz 300 in Florida. She toured the country to promote her album and appeared at several NASCAR events. These were a thrill for Kellie, who loves fast cars and has always been a big fan of stock car racing.

'I Wonder,' a bittersweet ballad to the mother who left Pickler when she was two, and 'My Angel,' a sentimental tribute to the grandmother who raised her, show that this small-town girl is someone the world should listen to."

Commercial Success

Small Town Girl was not only a critical success but it proved to be a commercial success as well. The top three singles from the album, "I Wonder," "Red High Heels," and "Things That Never Cross a Man's Mind," each made it to the top 20 on *Billboard*'s Hot Country Songs chart. Each song sold hundreds of thousands of copies in digital downloads. The album itself debuted in top place on *Billboard*'s Top Country Albums chart and went on to sell nearly 800,000 copies, earning Kellie a gold record—a designation reserved for albums that sell more than a half-million copies.

Kellie spent much of 2007 on tour promoting the album. She served as the opening act for the hit country group Rascal Flatts and performed the national anthem at the Daytona 500 in Florida, the top NASCAR race of the year.

NASCAR, KELLIE, AND KELLY

Kellie Pickler is a big fan of stock car racing. In America, big-time stock car racing is sanctioned by the National Association for Stock Car Auto Racing (NASCAR). When NASCAR was founded in the 1940s, most of the races were held at tracks throughout the South, which explains why the sport has earned such widespread appeal among southerners.

Another *American Idol* celebrity, season one winner Kelly Clarkson, is also a big NASCAR fan. Kelly has performed at several NASCAR pre-race concerts and even got to try her hand at driving a race car at the Daytona International Speedway in Florida. Kellie, who has also performed the National Anthem at NASCAR races, grew up near the Lowe's Motor Speedway in North Carolina and has always been a fan of stock car racing. "I love cars and I love fast cars," she says.

She also performed at the Grand Old Opry House, the 4,000-seat auditorium in Nashville where virtually every major star in the history of country music has played. "As soon as I pulled into the Opry House parking lot, before I even got out of my car, I was on cloud nine," Kellie said. "I've always dreamed of singing at the Opry." It seems that wherever Kellie performed, she found enthusiastic fans. Said Joe Galante, chairman of Kellie's label, Sony BMG Nashville,

> **"She's a very special lady in terms of her personality. . . . [Fans] can relate. People know her, but they also like her, and they are willing to spend their hard-earned money to hear more about her."**

Street-Smart, Not Book-Smart

Kellie may have been riding atop a wave of popularity, but one of her personal appearances created the type of publicity she has had trouble living down. In November 2007, Kellie appeared on the Fox show *Are You Smarter Than a 5th Grader?* As the name suggests, contestants are teamed with fifth-grade students, known as "classmates," in a quiz competition that poses the type of questions fifth-grade students are expected to answer correctly. The show often takes a humorous turn because the adult contestants frequently stumble over questions that their younger classmates answer in a breeze.

Kellie appeared during a celebrity week on the show to help raise money for two charities, but her best intentions were soon forgotten as she missed the answer to a very simple question: Budapest is the capital of what European country? Stumped by the question, Kellie admitted that she didn't know and, in fact, believed Europe was a country (and not a continent). When she was told the answer—Hungary—she found that answer hard to believe, mispronouncing the country as "Hungry" and telling the audience that she never heard of that country, either, although she

Kellie charms her audience during the Academy of Country Music New Artists' Party for a Cause show in 2007. One reason for Kellie's success is that she makes her fans feel like they know her. When she sings, fans always want to hear more.

did know about the country named Turkey. Later, the *New York Times* discussed Kellie's stumble over basic European geography in a story published under the headline, "Dumb and Dumber: Are Americans Hostile to Knowledge?"

Kellie's flub became the hit of the Internet and also prompted many observers of popular culture to compare her to Jessica Simpson, another popular and talented singer who has a reputation for speaking first and thinking later. For her part, Kellie is

Jessica Simpson (left) joins Kellie at the 44th Academy of Country Music Awards nominations. Some people have compared the two because they have made vocabulary and geography mistakes during public appearances. Kellie has taken this in stride, saying she is intelligent, but perhaps not "book-smart."

a bit perturbed that she has been the subject of national ridicule while the good she did on the show—raising $50,000 for charity—has gone virtually unnoticed. She says,

JESSICA SIMPSON'S VOCABULARY

Jessica Simpson has recorded hit albums, starred in films, made the covers of magazines, and dated quarterback Tony Romo, but when she opens her mouth it's anybody's guess what will come out. So when Kellie started skewering the English language, it didn't take long for the media to start comparing her to Jessica Simpson.

Jessica's most famous flub may have occurred when she thought she knew the difference between vowels and consonants. Or was it vowels and continents? She said, "A teacher asked us if anybody knew the names of the continents. I was sooo excited. I was like. . . . It's my first day of seventh grade, I'm in junior high and I know this answer. So I raised my hand, I was the first one, and I said A-E-I-O-U!"

She also turned down Buffalo wings because she thought they were actually made of buffalo meat. Of course, they are really spicy chicken wings, called Buffalo wings because the recipe originated in Buffalo, New York. And when appearing on the VH1 Awards show in 2005, she had a rather "emotional" experience when she said, "Isn't it weird I'm getting all *emotionable*."

"It kind of rubs me the wrong way. . . that people made such a big deal about that. I was there to win money for my charities and I won [$50,000] for my charities. I was there for a good cause, and none of that was publicized. . . . I'm not stupid. I think I'm very intelligent; maybe I'm not book-smart, but I'm street-smart."

Kellie has always believed in herself and her music, as she showed on her second, self-titled album. Many of her songs offer personal messages to young girls who, like Kellie, have needed to draw on their inner strength in times of trouble.

5

Believing in Herself

Kellie's second album, the self-titled *Kellie Pickler*, seemed to pick up where *Small Town Girl* left off. Released in the fall of 2008, the album scored strong sales as well as critical praise. Like *Small Town Girl*, *Kellie Pickler* included songs with strong personal messages, particularly the single "Don't You Know You're Beautiful."

The song is a tribute to women and girls who often suffer through moments of self-doubt, offering words of encouragement to three characters in the song: a wayward teenager, a homecoming queen losing her innocence, and a wife abandoned by her husband. Wrote a critic for Great American Country TV network,

“‘Don’t You Know You’re Beautiful,’ is more than a song, it’s a statement from Kellie Pickler, who chose the upbeat tune to lead off her self-titled second album. Urging inner strength, independence and confidence, the first single from *Kellie Pickler* introduces Kellie as she is today, a resilient young woman who has wrestled with insecurity, endured tragedy, suffered heartbreak and celebrated triumph on a winding road to maturity, self-awareness and newfound happiness.”

In 2009 Kellie’s video of the song would earn her a nomination for Country Music Television’s Female Video of the Year.

Busy Tour Schedule

Like Kellie’s first album, *Kellie Pickler* debuted in top place on *Billboard*’s country chart. Since its release, the album has recorded strong sales, selling more than 200,000 copies.

Kellie would find herself on tour for much of 2008, making more than 200 appearances before audiences. One of the highlights of her touring schedule that year was the annual Country Thunder Festival in Twin Lakes, Wisconsin. Another came a few months later in Nashville when she co-hosted, along with country stars Taylor Swift and Julianne Hough, the *Country Music Association Music Festival: Country’s Night to Rock*, which was nationally telecast. (Julianne, by the way, found stardom in country music the same way as Kellie—on a reality TV show. In Julianne’s case, she won first place in the 2007 and 2008 seasons of *Dancing with the Stars.*)

In addition to the 2008 Country Music Television awards and ASCAP honors she had garnered for “I Wonder,” Kellie was also nominated that year for awards from the Academy of Country Music for Top New Female Vocalist of the Year and the Country Music Association for the Horizon Award, which is now known as New Artist of the Year.

As Kellie was touring, her embarrassing episode on *Are You Smarter Than a 5th Grader?* caught up with her, but this time she shared in the laugh. She encountered some fans from Hungary, who gave her a special gift: a Hungarian flag.

Another Small Town Girl

A prior winner of the Horizon Award is Carrie Underwood. Carrie has helped pave the way for Kellie and other country singers to be regarded as serious competitors on *Idol.* Before Carrie entered the competition, pop singers like Kelly Clarkson and Clay Aiken as well as rhythm and blues singers like Ruben Studdard, Fantasia Barrino, and Jennifer Hudson dominated

Kellie encourages a packed audience to clap along as she performs on her 2008 tour. In spite of her busy touring schedule, she found time to co-host the Country Music Association Music Festival and receive nominations for several country music awards.

the competition. But when Carrie auditioned before Simon, Randy, and Paula, her performance showed that country singers could also gain critical support from the judges and, eventually, widespread fan appeal. Before Carrie auditioned, even Simon admitted to being somewhat surprised that country singers had yet to make an impact on the show. After Carrie's tryout, he said, "I'm surprised we haven't found a good country singer in this competition."

After Kellie left *Idol*, she developed a close friendship with Carrie. The two stars have similar backgrounds: both grew

Country singer and *American Idol* season four winner Carrie Underwood has become a close friend of Kellie's. Both grew up as small-town girls; they also share similar high school and early work experiences, a vegetarian lifestyle, and a dedication to country music.

up in small towns in rural America (Carrie was raised in Checotah, Oklahoma); both were high school cheerleaders and beauty pageant contestants; both worked as waitresses; and both dedicated themselves to country music. Carrie has even convinced Kellie to become a vegetarian. For Kellie, maintaining a vegetarian lifestyle has often been difficult, but she has relied heavily on Carrie's guidance. She says,

CARRIE UNDERWOOD

Kellie's friend Carrie Underwood did not plan for a career in music but instead hoped to find a job in broadcast journalism. Born in 1983 in rural Oklahoma, Carrie was always musically talented and occasionally performed before audiences. But she never really got serious about music until just before beginning her final semester in college when she heard *American Idol* would be auditioning contestants. Carrie drove eight hours to St. Louis, Missouri, to try out for the show and was picked to go to Hollywood. She ended up skipping her last semester to be able to compete—although she later returned to Northeastern State University in Oklahoma to earn her degree—and went on to win the competition.

Since winning the competition in the fourth season of *Idol*, Carrie has released two best-selling albums, *Some Hearts* and *Carnival Ride*. Both albums have been certified as platinum, meaning they have each sold more than a million copies. Even though Carrie grew up on an Oklahoma cattle ranch, she is an avowed **vegetarian**, meaning she refuses to eat meat. She is also a dedicated activist for animal rights, and has helped raise money for the Humane Society of the United States.

"Most country girls do like their meat! I used to eat steak rare all the time. I'd just throw it on the grill for two seconds, flip it over and it was done and everyone was like, 'That's so gross—that thing is still moving!' . . . So [Carrie and I] have this little

vegetarian thing going on. I'll text her and be like, 'Is fish considered a meat?' And she'll be like, 'Well, different people look at it differently.'"

Romance and Bad Reunions

Kellie has also made friends with Taylor Swift, who helped Kellie get over a difficult time in her life. Even as Kellie found success on the record charts her personal life was in turmoil. Soon after moving to Nashville Kellie met and started dating Nashville Predators hockey star Jordin Tootoo.

For a time, Kellie and Jordin seemed to be inseparable. Kellie could be found attending the Predators games—occasionally accompanied by Carrie and Taylor. She said, "I scream my head off in a Predators jersey at his games, and he comes to my concerts and does the same." Kellie also accompanied Jordin on a trip to his hometown in Rankin Inlet, which is located just below the **Arctic Circle** in northern Canada. When she arrived in the community, she found the Tootoo family living in a rural cabin with few modern luxuries. In an interview with the Canadian Broadcasting Company, Kellie said,

"[There's] no cell phone service here, so that's a big plus. No one probably knows what a cell phone is here. . . . I've had different types of food that I never in my wildest dreams ever thought I'd try—raw caribou and whale blubber. You've got to salt everything."

For months, the **tabloid** press followed the romance between Kellie and Jordin, but the two eventually broke up. Meanwhile, Kellie's father Bo got out of jail. Kellie and Bo made attempts to reconnect, but Bo eventually found himself in trouble again and was sent back to jail. Kellie's wayward mother Cynthia also showed up—that was the incident that prompted Kellie to lose her composure

Kellie (right) and country singing star Taylor Swift arrive at the 2007 American Music Awards. Kellie became friends with Taylor, who helped her deal with depression and collaborated with her on a song that gives advice on how to get over bad breakups. Later Kellie also joined Taylor on her tour.

at the Country Music Awards. Efforts by Kellie and her mother to reconnect failed as well. The pain of her breakup with Tootoo and the reappearances of her mother and father caused Kellie to suffer much anguish. She soon fell into a period of depression.

Battling Depression

Depression is a mental illness that interferes with the ability to work, study, sleep, and otherwise enjoy life. Depressed people may lack the energy to get out of bed in the morning. People who are depressed also suffer from high rates of suicide.

Taylor helped Kellie get over her depression, mostly by working with her on a song for the *Kellie Pickler* album, "Best Days of Your Life," which gives girls advice on how to get over bad breakups with their boyfriends. Taylor also appears in the video for the song. Says Kellie,

> **"When I hang out with Taylor, I don't get in any trouble. On New Year's Eve, we baked cakes and she taught me the Soulja Boy dance in her kitchen. Her dancing has really improved."**

TAYLOR SWIFT

Still a teenager in 2008, Taylor Swift achieved the distinction of being the top-selling musical star of the year with two albums, *Taylor Swift* and *Fearless*, selling more than 4 million copies. When *Fearless*, her second album, was released in late 2008, *Billboard* magazine said,

> **"Those who thought Swift was a big deal after her first record should be prepared: She's about to get way bigger. . . . Swift's songs have broad appeal, and therein lies the genius and accessibility of *Fearless.* The insightful 'Fifteen' ('In your life you'll do greater things than dating a boy on the football team . . . ') will connect with teens looking for hope and with adult women looking back."**

Born in 1989, Taylor grew up near Reading, Pennsylvania. She began singing at the age of 10 and, a year later, traveled to Nashville with the hope of signing a record deal. She was unable to interest a label in her talent, but three years later her family moved to the Nashville area so Taylor could pursue her interest in country music full time. Eventually, the strategy paid off and at the age of 17 Taylor signed with a label.

Kellie also started a new romantic relationship with Nashville songwriter Kyle Jacobs, and she credits Kyle with helping her get over her depression as well.

USO Tour

Working hard with Taylor and other talented people to produce *Kellie Pickler* helped Kellie shake her blues. She also found that maintaining a busy tour schedule kept her active, and when she was active she didn't have time to be sad and depressed.

Kellie entertains soldiers during a 2008 USO tour. She proudly performed for over 20,000 men and women serving in the Middle East. Kellie had done a previous USO tour in 2007 and says she never takes for granted what those troops do for their country.

Kellie joins Kid Rock in a musical number during her USO tour in 2008. Kellie is just one of many entertainers who continue the more than 60-year-old USO tradition of entertaining armed forces members who serve their country far from home.

In late 2008, Kellie embarked on a busy tour schedule as she volunteered to participate in a USO show that entertained American troops in Europe and the Middle East—Germany, Great Britain, Kosovo, Afghanistan, and Iraq. It was something of a whirlwind tour—nine shows were staged in just five days, with Kellie performing before more than 20,000 troops. It was actually the second time that Kellie had flown overseas on a USO tour—she made her first tour of American military bases in late 2007. Said Kellie,

> **"Seeing the faces of over 20,000 military men and women—that is forever printed on my mind. Once again, the most incredible thing I have ever done in my life. . . . Thank you, thank you, to the men and women serving our country. I will never take what you do for granted."**

ENTERTAINING THE TROOPS

Kellie Pickler joined a long tradition of celebrities who volunteer to entertain American troops when she participated in United Service Organizations (USO) tours in 2007 and 2008. The USO was formed in 1941 just prior to World War II. During the war the USO established many centers to provide places where soldiers and sailors could find entertainment and meals as they trained for combat away from home.

The USO's best-known activity is staging shows for members of the American military serving overseas. For decades, Hollywood stars, pop singers, comics, and other entertainers have volunteered to perform in shows at American bases, many in close proximity to war zones. The late comedian and movie star Bob Hope hosted many of those shows, making his first appearance at a U.S. Army base in Alaska in 1942, nine months after America's entry into World War II. Hope made his last appearance in front of troops serving in the Persian Gulf War in 1990 and 1991. At the time, Hope was 87 years old. He died in 2003 at the age of 100.

Kellie is thrilled to join her idol Dolly Parton on stage during a charity event to raise money for musical instruments in Nashville schools. Kellie said of Dolly, "There isn't anything she can't do." The same can be said of Kellie, as she keeps believing in herself and looking toward a bright future in music.

Joining Dolly and Taylor

Kellie remained busy throughout 2009, starting off the year working as an entertainment reporter at the **Super Bowl**, providing televised reports for *The Tonight Show with Jay Leno*, then performing with her idol, Dolly Parton, as the two stars took part in a Gift of Music charity event in Nashville. The event helped raise money to buy musical instruments for the W.O. Smith Community School. At the event, staged at the Wildhorse Saloon in Nashville, Kellie sang some of her hits, then performed a duet with Dolly on the song "9 to 5," which Dolly wrote for the 1980 film *Nine to Five*, in which she starred. The song humorously describes the toils of the American working class. Shortly after their performance together, Kellie said of Dolly,

> **"I don't think there's anything that woman can't do. She just walks into a room and lights it up. She's got that 'it' factor that money can't buy."**

Following her duet with Dolly, Kellie joined Taylor for the national tour for her album, *Fearless*. With her depression behind her and big plans on the horizon, Kellie has resolved to believe in herself and continue performing. She says,

> **"I did *American Idol* in 2006. . . . It's amazing how fast time has flown by and how much has happened in just that little, short amount of time. The biggest adjustment is how much your life does change. It's so much to take in and absorb. But this is what I've wanted my whole life, and I finally got it. So I'm definitely going to take advantage of every opportunity that comes along."**

1986 Kellie Pickler is born in Albemarle, North Carolina, on June 28.

1988 Moves in with her grandparents, Clyde and Faye Pickler, after her parents separate.

2002 *American Idol* premiers on the Fox network.

Grandmother Faye Pickler dies.

2004 Graduates from North Stanly High School in New London, North Carolina.

Enrolls in Stanly Community College and studies cosmetology.

2005 Auditions for *American Idol* and is selected to compete in Hollywood.

2006 Voted off *American Idol* on April 26, finishing in sixth place.

Appears for the first time on the stage of the Grand Ole Opry in Nashville on October 27.

Releases her first album, *Small Town Girl,* on October 31.

2007 *Small Town Girl* certified gold on January 18.

Loses her composure while performing "I Wonder" at the Country Music Awards on November 7, but later wins an award from Country Music Television for the performance.

On November 17, flubs the answers on *Are You Smarter Than a 5th Grader* but raises $50,000 for charity.

2008 The album *Kellie Picker* is released on September 30.

Tours Germany, Great Britain, Afghanistan, Iraq, and Kosovo with the USO.

2009 Performs with Dolly Parton on February 2 at a charity fundraiser in Nashville.

Joins Taylor Swift on her *Fearless* tour.

Awards, Nominations, and Recognition

2004 Wins Miss Stanly County, North Carolina, beauty pageant.

2008 "I Wonder" and "Red High Heels" recognized as Most Performed Songs by ASCAP.

"I Wonder" voted winner of the Country Music Television Breakthrough Video of the Year and Tearjerker Video of the Year.

Kellie's tearful performance of "I Wonder" at the Country Music Awards show voted Country Music Television's Performance of the Year.

Nominated by the Academy of Country Music for Top New Female Vocalist of the Year.

Nominated by the Country Music Association for the Horizon Award.

2009 Kellie's performance of "Don't You Know You're Beautiful" nominated for the Country Music Television award for Female Video of the Year.

Albums

2006 *Small Town Girl*

2008 *Kellie Pickler*

Hit Singles

2006 "Red High Heels"

2007 "I Wonder"

"Things That Never Cross a Man's Mind"

2008 "Don't You Know You're Beautiful"

"Best Days of Your Life"

Arctic Circle—Last major line of latitude south of the North Pole.

Broadway—Street in New York City where most major live-performance theaters are located; typically, the term is used for any major stage play performed in New York.

cosmetologist—Professional who cuts and styles hair.

genre—Category of pieces of music that share a certain style or theme.

labels—Music recording companies, so known because in the era of vinyl records their names would appear on the round paper labels pasted to the centers of the records.

lyrics—Words that tell the story of the song; the lyrics are performed by the singer and set to the melody and beat of the music.

naïveté—Sincere or natural simplicity.

paralegal—Professional who assists a lawyer, often by researching and drafting legal documents and interviewing witnesses.

satellite hookup—Communications relay that uses satellites orbiting in space; typically, a TV or radio signal is beamed to the satellite, which then relays the signal to a receiver in a distant place on earth.

studio audience—Audience members who witness a live performance in a TV studio that is transmitted live, or later on tape, to viewers at home.

Super Bowl—National Football League championship game, typically staged each year in early February.

tabloid—Style of journalism practiced in newspapers, TV, and the Internet that focuses on celebrity news and gossip and bizarre crimes; popularized during the 1920s by newspapers published in tabloid format, meaning they were half the size of broadsheet newspapers.

tuition—Cost of attending college or private school.

vegetarian—Person who has elected, on moral principles, not to eat meat.

Books

Cowell, Simon. *I Don't Mean to be Rude, But . . .* New York: Broadway Books, 2003.

Kallen, Stuart A. *The History of Country Music.* Farmington Hills, Michigan: Lucent, 2002.

McGuire, Jim. *Nashville Portraits: Legends of Country Music.* Guilford, Connecticut: Globe Piquot, 2007.

Miller, Stephen. *Smart Blonde: Dolly Parton.* London, England: Omnibus Press, 2008.

Periodicals

Huff, Richard. "Never an 'Idol' Moment for Kellie." *New York Daily News* (May 18, 2008): p. 5.

Spelling, Ian. "Kellie Pickler is Enjoying the Ride; *Idol* Contender Hasn't Slowed Down." *Bergen County Record* (January 18, 2008): p. G-12.

Tauber, Michelle. "Kellie's Wild Ride." *People* vol. 66, no. 20 (November 15, 2006): p. 89.

Tucker, Ken. "Getting to Know Her." *Billboard* vol. 120, no. 37 (September 13, 2008): p. 59.

Web Sites

www.americanidol.com

On *American Idol*'s official Web site, fans can read biographies of the competitors, view photos and videos, and read the latest news about the show and the performers. By accessing the site's Alumni News link, fans can find updates for many of the performers in *American Idol*'s past seasons.

www.ascap.com

Students can learn about the American Society of Composers, Authors, and Publishers (ASCAP) by visiting the organization's Web site. By accessing the ASCAP History link, students can find a decade by decade history of ASCAP, tracing the group's roots back nearly a century to its founding by some of America's most noted songwriters and composers.

www.cmt.com

Country Music Television, the TV network devoted to country and western music, maintains a Web site that includes many resources for fans, including news about performers, tour dates, photos, and lyrics from many current hits. The site also includes extensive biographies of many country stars, including Kellie.

www.kelliepickler.com

Kellie's official Web site includes news, updates on her tour schedule, photos, and blogs where fans can add their comments. Fans can also view videos and download wallpaper for their home computers.

PICTURE CREDITS

page

2: BNA/19 Recordings/NMI
8: Laura Farr/AdMedia Photos
11: ASCAP/PRMS
13: Kevin Winter/Getty Images
14: Great American Country/PRMS
14: (insert) Fox Network/PRMS
17: New Millennium Images
18: Fox Network/PRMS
20: Fox Network/PRMS
23: Fox Network/PRMS
24: Fox Network/PRMS
27: 19 Entertainment/NMI
28: RCA Records/NMI
31: Ray Mickshaw/WireImage
32: Fox Network/PRMS
34: BNA/19 Recordings/NMI
37: BNA/19 Recordings/NMI
38: Jamie Squire/NASCAR/PRMS
41: Ethan Miller/Getty Images
42: Donn Jones/Splash News
44: BNA/19 Recordings/NMI
47: Splash News and Pictures
48: Arista/19 Recordings/NMI
51: Michael Buckner/AMA/PRMS
53: Chad J. McNeeley/U.S. Navy/NMI
54: Chad J. McNeeley/U.S. Navy/NMI
56: StageShottz Magazine

Front cover: Fox Network/PRMS
Front cover insert: Fox Network/PRMS

ABOUT THE AUTHOR

Hal Marcovitz is a former newspaper reporter who has written more than 100 books for young readers. In 2005, *Nancy Pelosi*, his biography of House Speaker Nancy Pelosi, was named to *Booklist* magazine's list of recommended feminist books for young readers. He lives in Chalfont, Pennsylvania, with his wife Gail and daughter Ashley.